bagan, barra barra, mirriwarr

The Boys Who Found Their Way

Tyran Uddin and Kayden Wellington, with Kirli Saunders and Jaz Corr

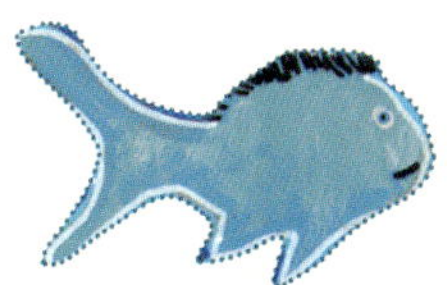

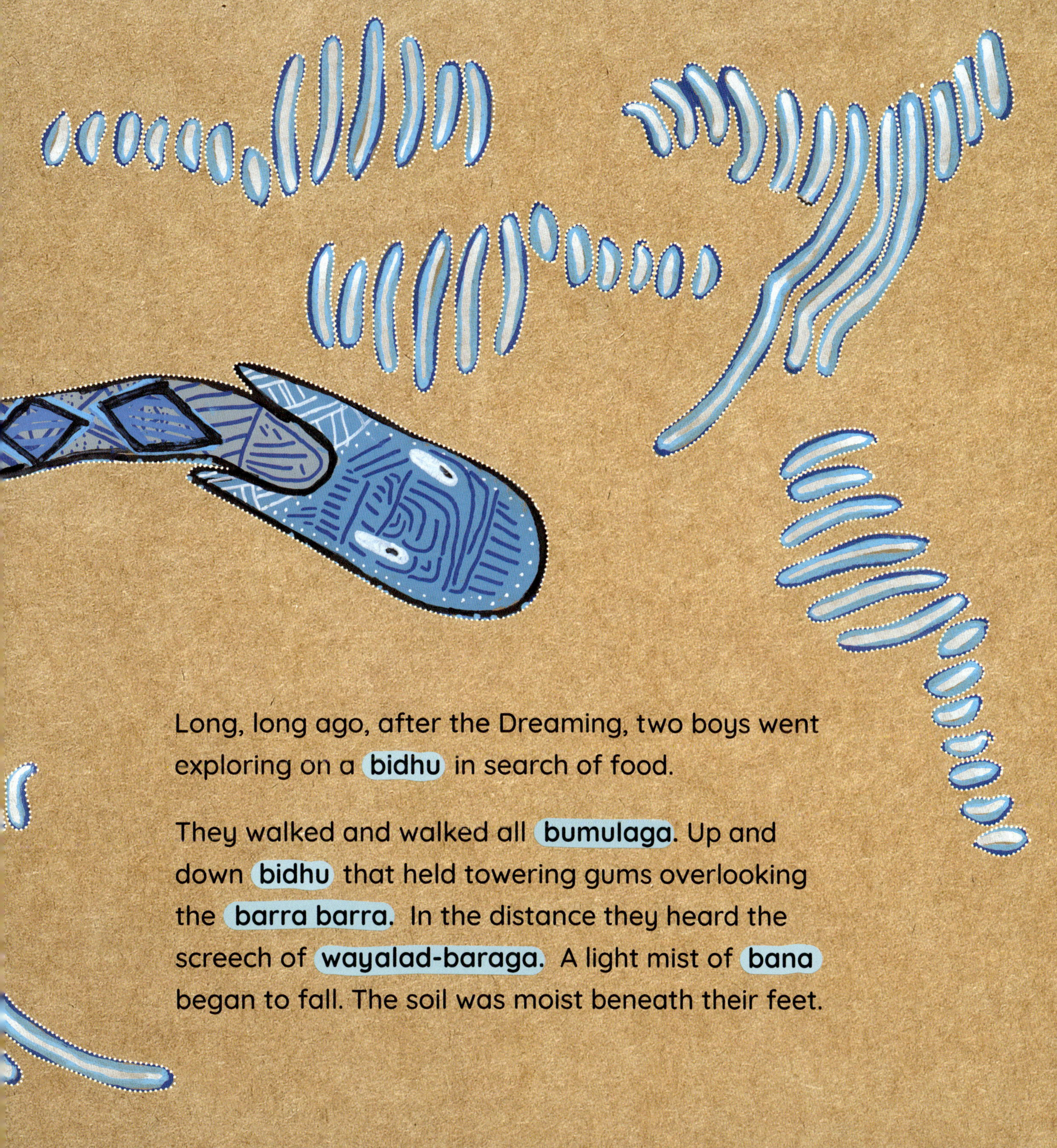

Long, long ago, after the Dreaming, two boys went exploring on a bidhu in search of food.

They walked and walked all bumulaga. Up and down bidhu that held towering gums overlooking the barra barra. In the distance they heard the screech of wayalad-baraga. A light mist of bana began to fall. The soil was moist beneath their feet.

At the base of the bidhu they began to collect purple berries when, all of a sudden, a Great Buru approached them and said, “Those berries are not yet ripe.”

The **Great Buru** jumped closer and said, “Follow me and learn about the land. Let’s go for a walk.”

Great Buru showed the boys different plants on the mountain. He explained the difference between edible and non-edible fruit. He explained the different seasons. He explained how to track animals for tucker by looking at their footprints – badhaalima, burnaaga, ganagubadh and birdhuulay. He explained the importance of ganji and showed them how to use it. Ganji is good for the bagan. Ganji gives us life. He taught the boys a dance that honours all life on the land.

Finally Great Buru told the boys that we must only ever take what we need because if we don't then there will be nothing left.

The boys thanked the Great Buru for teaching them about the land. The Great Buru took the boys to the barra barra and called upon the Great Muriyira.

Suddenly the Great Muriyira emerged from the sea and said,

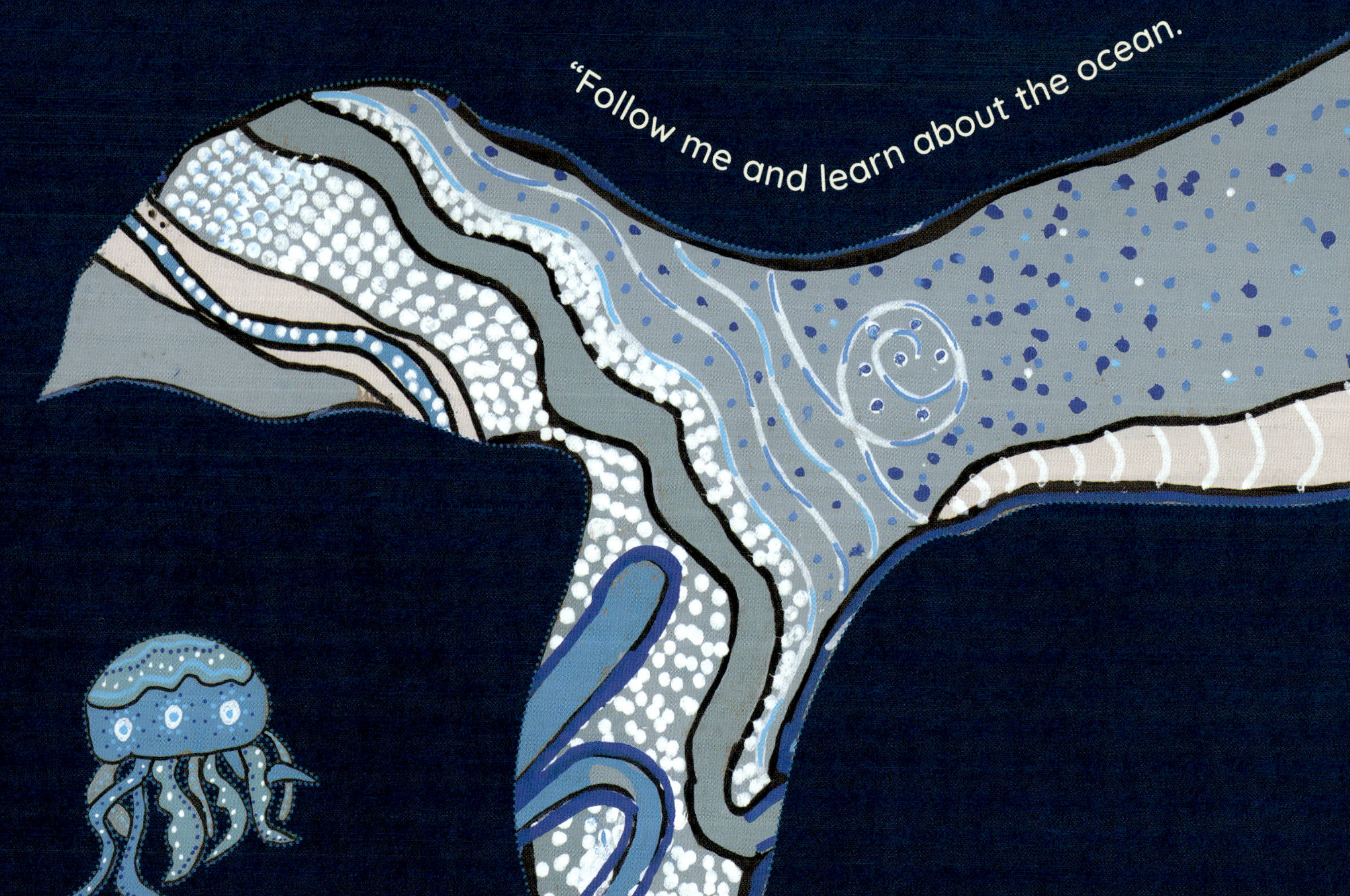

Hold onto my back, let's explore the **barra barra.**"

marra
bidhanga
baba

The Great Muriyira showed the boys the different marra in the barra barra. She explained that some marra are poisonous and some marra are not. She explained the migration of different species – warrabugan, warigala, barraaran and dhagala. She explained how to catch marra with garawad, nets and traps. She explained that when spearing marra you need to be one with the barra barra. She taught the boys a dance which honours all life in the ocean.

Finally she told them that we must only ever take what we need because if we don't then there will be nothing left.

The boys thanked the Great Muriyira for teaching them about the sea. The Great Muriyira took them back to shore and called upon the **Great Marida.**

The Great Muriyira showed them the **bunbal** on the land where the Great Marida lives. The boys walked over to the **bunbal**.

When the boys got there the Great Marida said, “Climb up my great tree and I will teach you about the laws of this land.”

Once the boys climbed to the top of bunbal the Great Marida explained that there are some boundaries where you cannot go. He explained that there are gimbanya-waraga and ngaranggal-baraga places. He explained that some places are very sacred and that no one should go there unless they have permission from the gamara-waraga ba muladha-waraga.

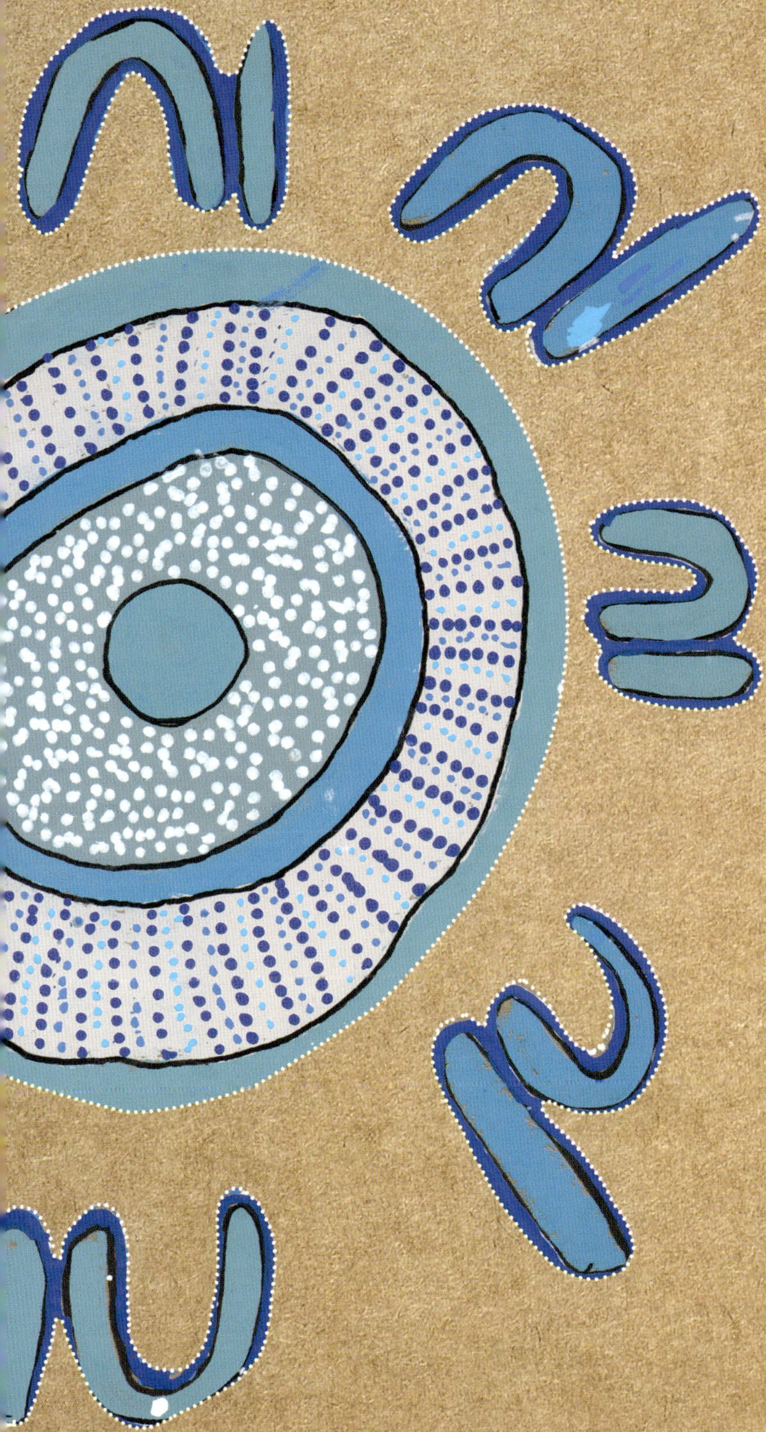

He finally explained that every person on this land has a totem: a sacred animal that you share a special relationship with forever. He explained that people should never eat their totems. He taught the boys a dance that honours these laws of the land.

The boys then carefully climbed down the tree with the Great Marida and thanked him for teaching them.

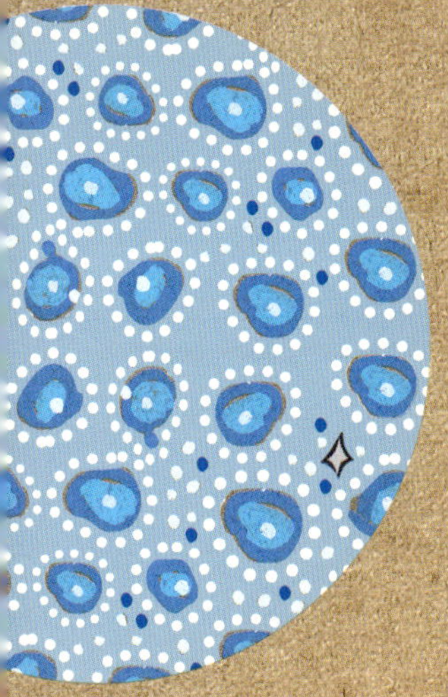

The Great Marida told them that we must only ever take what we need because if we don't then there will be nothing left.

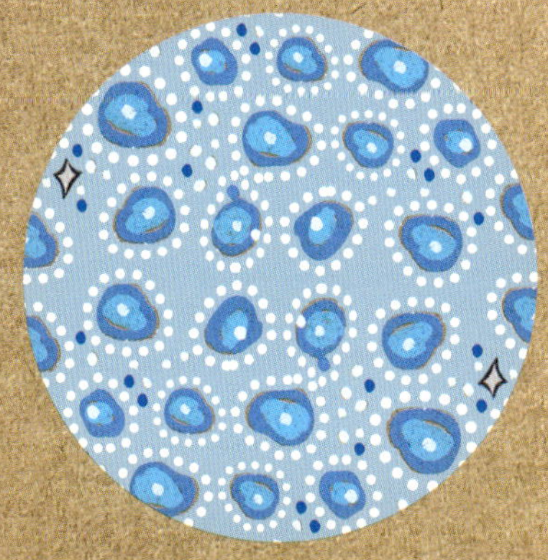

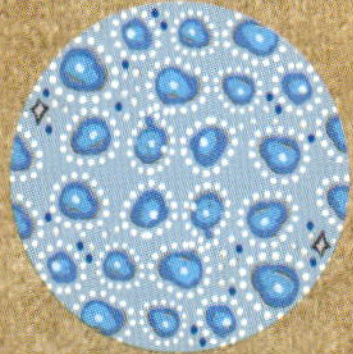

The boys began their journey **munggura.**
Walking down the **djaadjawan** and then over the **bidhu,** underneath a forest of **bunbal-baraga** that **milumba** with wisdom in the **baliya.**

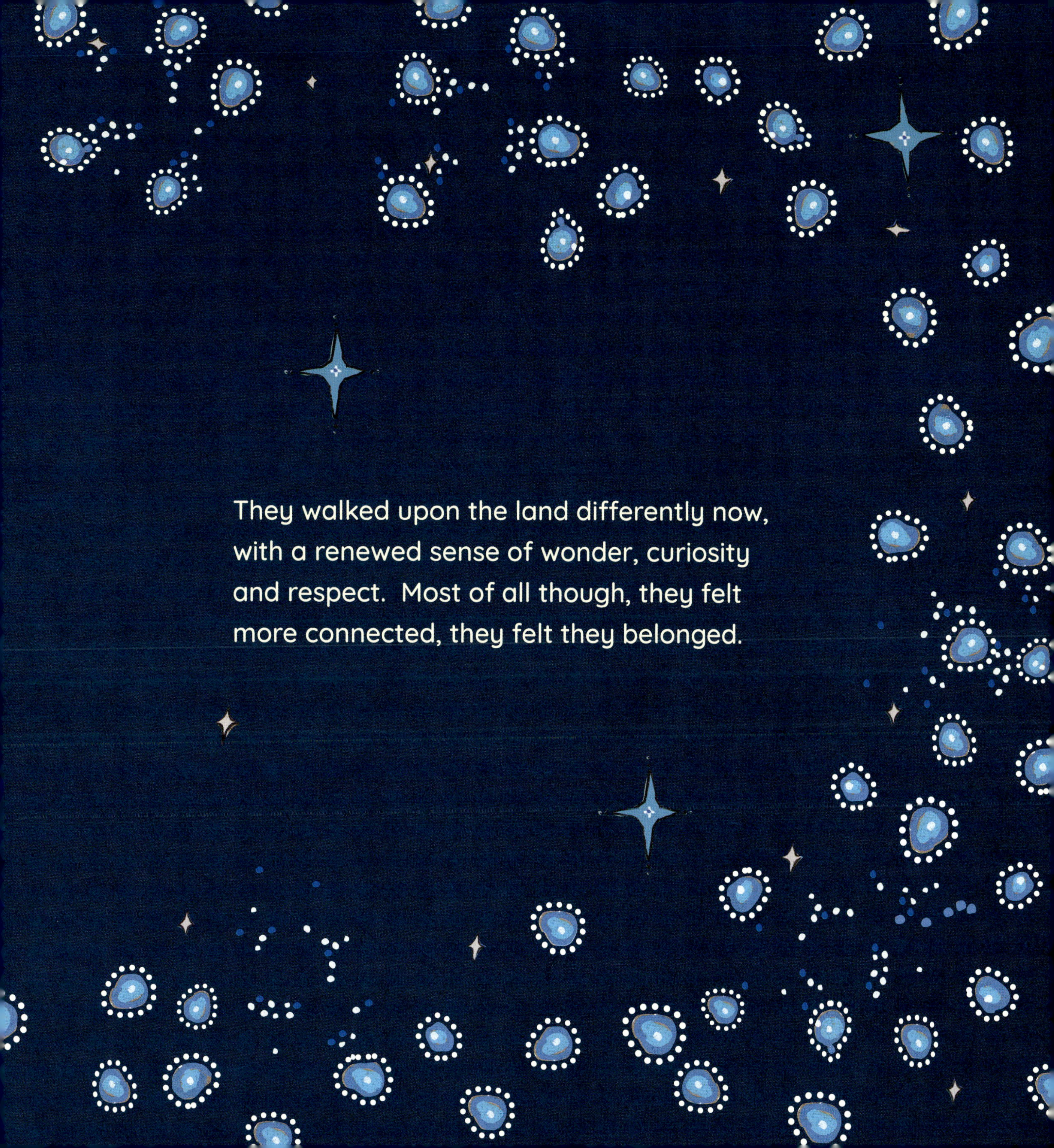

They walked upon the land differently now, with a renewed sense of wonder, curiosity and respect. Most of all though, they felt more connected, they felt they belonged.

When the boys got **munggura,** they told their family all about their adventure. They shared the knowledge they had learnt that day, and for the rest of their lives they followed the rules and taught their **yuwinj** the way.

Glossary

ba and

badhaalima wallaby

bagan earth

baliya north east wind

bana rain

barra barra sea

barraaran snapper

bidhu mountain

birdhuulay bandicoot

bumulaga morning

bunbal tree

bunbal-baraga trees

burnaaga goanna

buru kangaroo

dhagala flathead

djaadjawan sand

gamara-waraga old men

ganagubadh echidna

ganji fire

garawad fishing spears

gimbanya-waraga men

marra fish

marida sea eagle

milumba shimmer

muladha-waraga old women / old people

munggura home

muriyira whale

ngaranggal-baraga women

warigala mullet

warrabugan whiting

wayalad-baraga black cockatoos

yuwinj Yuin people

First published in 2024 by the Indigenous Literacy Foundation
Gadigal Country, Level 17/207 Kent Street
Sydney NSW 2000
ilf.org.au

Reprinted 2025

Cataloguing-in-Publication details are available from the National Library of Australia

www.trove.nla.gov.au

ISBN: 9781923179219

Typesetting and design by Mary Callahan

Printed by RR Donnelly Asia Printing Solutions Limited

This project was supported by First Sentier Investors

marra
bidhanga
wulimbura
baba